CAPRICORN SUN

SYMBOL: SEAGOAT / ELEMENT: EARTH / RULING PLANET: SATURN / POWER COLOR: GRAY

December 22 – January 19

Shonette Charles

Copyright © 2023 by Shonette Charles.

All rights reserved. No part of this publication may be reproduced, distributed, or transmitted in any form or by any means, including photocopying, recording, or other electronic or mechanical methods, without the prior written permission of the publisher, except in the case of brief quotations embodied in critical reviews and certain other noncommercial uses permitted by copyright law. For permission requests, write to the publisher.

Seamare Press LLC
PO Box 99095
Raleigh, NC 27624
www.seamarepress.com

Quantity sales. Special discounts are available on quantity purchases by corporations, associations, and others. For details, contact the address above.

Capricorn Sun Vibes / Shonette Charles. — 1st ed.
ISBN 978-1-955689-30-4

Published in the United States of America by Seamare Press, Raleigh, NC.

YOUR ENERGY FIELDS

The human energy field is a complex and dynamic system of energy that surrounds and permeates our physical body. It is made up of several different layers, each of which corresponds to different aspects of our being. Understanding the different layers of the human energy field and how they work can help us to develop greater awareness and sensitivity to the subtle energies that shape our reality.

PHYSICAL
The most dense and tangible layer, it is closely connected to the physical body and is responsible for the overall health and vitality of the body. Influenced by nutrition, exercise, and environmental toxins.

ETHERIC
Subtle and dynamic, it surrounds and interpenetrates the physical layer and is responsible for the vital life force energy that animates the body. Influenced by stress, trauma, and energy blockages.

EMOTIONAL
Dynamic and ever-changing layer, it is closely connected to our emotional experiences and patterns and responsible for the energy of our emotions. Influenced by emotional trauma, repressed emotions, and emotional expression.

MENTAL
Complex and abstract layer, it is closely connected to our thoughts and beliefs and responsible for the energy of our mental processes. Influenced by limiting beliefs, negative self-talk, and mental clarity.

SPIRITUAL
The most expansive and subtle layer, it is closely connected to our spiritual practices and beliefs and responsible for the energy of our spiritual experiences. Influenced by meditation, prayer, and connection to a higher power.

Conscious vs Subconscious

While the conscious and the subconscious are distinct aspects of our mental processes, they are also interconnected and can influence each other in complex ways. For example, our subconscious beliefs and desires can influence our conscious thoughts and actions, while our conscious experiences can shape our subconscious processing and perception of the world.

conscious

- Awareness: Our immediate awareness of our surroundings, thoughts, and emotions
- Control: Has a sense of control over our thoughts and actions
- Processing: Active and deliberate processing of information
- Capacity: Limited, as we can only focus on a limited amount of information at any given time
- Will: Closely linked to our sense of free will and known desires

subconscious

- Awareness: Mental processes that are not immediately accessible to our conscious awareness
- Control: Operates outside of our conscious control and can influence our behavior in ways that we may not be aware of
- Processing: Automatic and passive processing of information
- Capacity: Greater capacity for processing and storing information
- Will: Can operate independently of our conscious intentions and desires

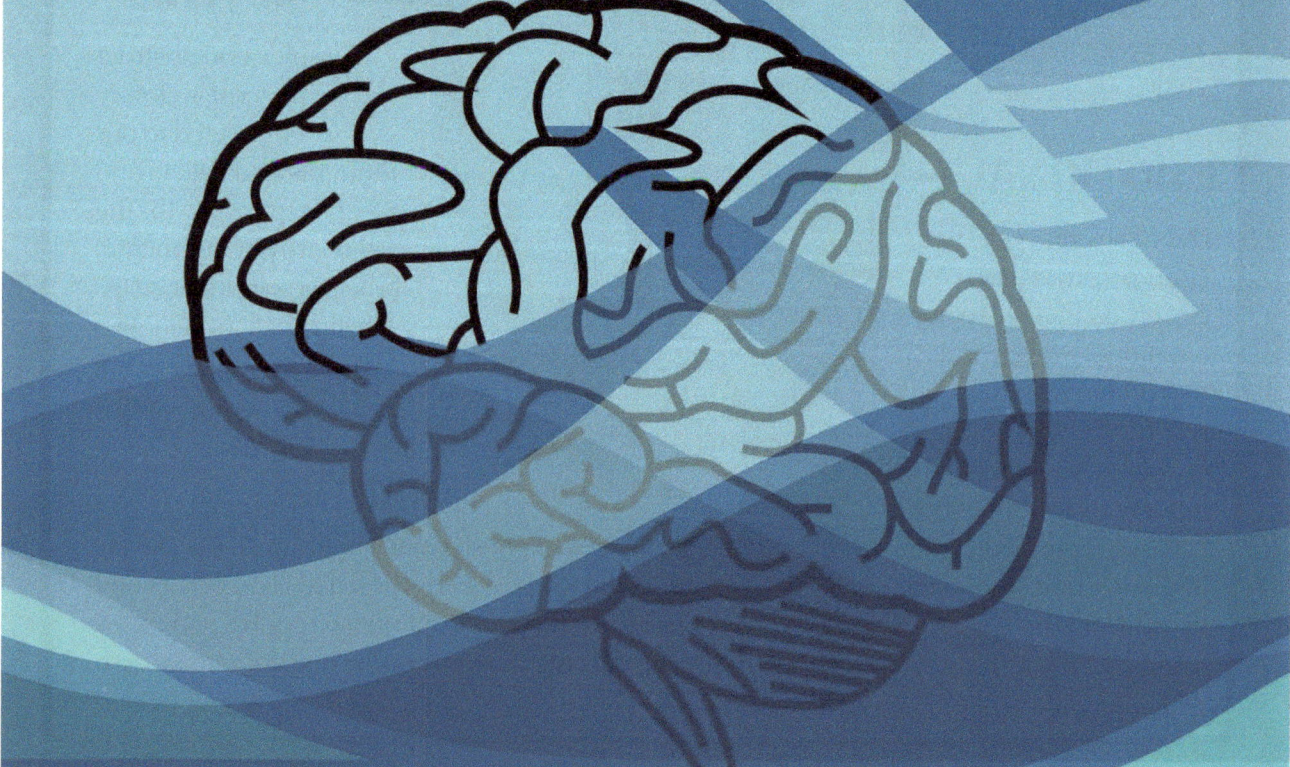

History of Astrology

The study of astrology has a long and rich history, with roots dating back thousands of years to ancient civilizations like Egypt, Babylon, and Greece. These cultures used astrology to help them understand the patterns and movements of the stars and planets, which they believed held important information about the world and their place in it. Over time, astrology evolved into a more complex system, incorporating ideas from philosophy, mythology, and mathematics.

During the Renaissance, astrology experienced a resurgence in popularity and was considered a respected field of study. However, with the rise of science and skepticism in the 17th and 18th centuries, astrology faced criticism and eventually fell out of favor with the mainstream. With the introduction of new technology making it easier to access and understand, there has been a resurgence in using astrology to better understand our personal energy and that of the world. Consequently, many find value in astrology as a tool for self-discovery and personal growth.

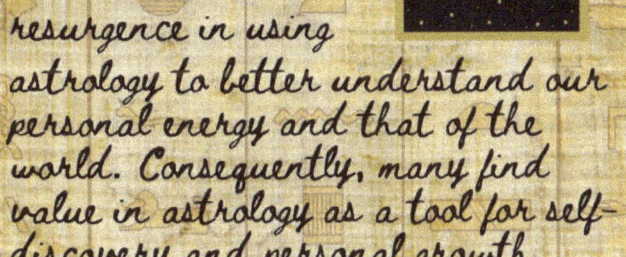

> "We are spiritual beings having a human experience."
> ~Pierre Teilhard de Chardin

SHONETTE CHARLES

Natal Chart

What is required of you:

- Birth Date
- Birth Time
- Birth City

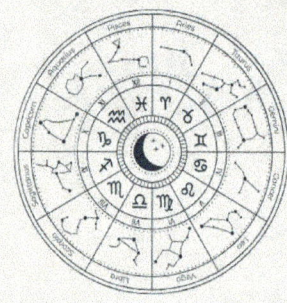

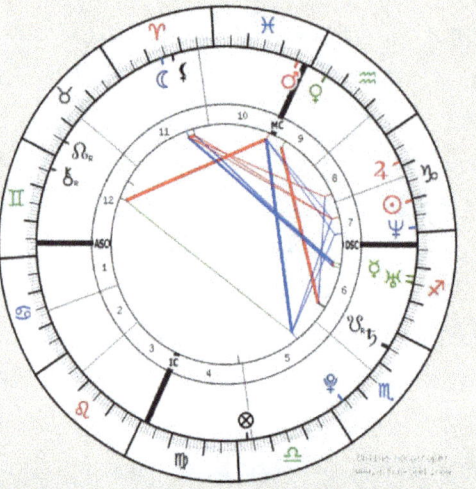

○ Sun
☽ Moon
☿ Mercury
♀ Venus
♂ Mars
♃ Jupiter
♄ Saturn
♅ Uranus
♆ Neptune
♇ Pluto

A natal chart is a map of the sky at the moment of your birth, showing the positions of the planets and other celestial bodies. Understanding your natal chart can provide insight into your energy, including strengths, weaknesses, and life purpose.

Step 1: Obtain your natal chart
There are many online websites that can generate your natal chart for free. Simply enter your birth date, time, and location to get an accurate chart.

Step 2: Identify the 12 houses
The natal chart is divided into 12 sections, called houses. Each house represents a different area of life, such as relationships, finances, career, and health.

Step 3: Identify the planets
The chart will show the positions of the sun, moon, and other planets at the time of your birth. Pay attention to the planets in your chart, the sign they are in, and their positions in the houses.

Step 4: Interpret the meaning of the planets
Each planet in astrology represents different qualities, such as love (Venus), communication (Mercury), and ambition (Mars). Look at where each planet is located in your chart, the sign, and what house it rules to understand its influence in your life.

Step 5: Study the aspects
The aspects in your natal chart show the relationships between the planets. Look at the angles between each planet and consider the meaning of the aspect. For example, a trine aspect is considered harmonious and supportive, while a square aspect is considered challenging.

Step 6: Look at your sun sign
Your sun sign is determined by the position of the sun in your chart at the time of your birth. This is the most well-known astrological sign and can provide insight into your basic energy.

Step 7: Reflect on what you've learned
Take some time to reflect on what you've learned from your natal chart. Consider what insights you've gained into yourself and your life path, and think about what steps you can take to nurture your strengths and work on your weaknesses.

Discover the Authentic You

Our authentic self is the truest expression of who we are as individuals, without the influence of external pressures or societal expectations. It is the part of ourselves that is most in tune with our deepest desires, values, and passions.

Living in alignment with our authentic self involves being true to ourselves, even if it means going against the norms or expectations of others. It involves embracing our unique strengths, talents, and quirks and expressing ourselves in a way that feels genuine and authentic.

When we are living in alignment with our authentic self, we experience a greater sense of fulfillment, meaning, and purpose in our lives. We feel more connected to ourselves and others, and we are able to tap into our innate creativity, intuition, and wisdom.

Exploring your natal chart can provide insight into your authentic self and help you better understand your natural energy. This guide is intended to help you with the process of discovering your authentic self.

Planet	Energy	Sign	House
Sun	how you express your core identity and individuality		
Moon	how you process and express your emotions.		
Rising	your outer personality, influencing first impressions, socializing		
Mercury	how you communicate and process information		
Venus	how you experience and express love, beauty, and pleasure		
Mars	how you assert yourself and pursue your goals		
Jupiter	where you seek growth and expansion in your life		
Saturn	where you experience limitations and challenges in your life		
Neptune	how you rebel against the norm and seek to express your unique self		
Uranus	where you experience creativity, spirituality, and inspiration		
Pluto	where you experience transformation, power, and change in your life		

When we don't live in alignment with our authentic selves, we experience a sense of disconnection, dissatisfaction, or even inner turmoil. Living out of alignment can manifest in a number of ways, including feeling unfulfilled in career or relationships, a sense of emptiness or lack of purpose, or constantly trying to fit in or meet the expectations of others, rather than expressing your true self.

Living inauthentically can also lead to physical and emotional symptoms, such as stress, anxiety, depression, or chronic health issues. When we are not living in alignment with our true selves, we may experience a sense of dis-ease or imbalance in our bodies and minds.

The good news is that it's never too late to realign with our authentic selves. By cultivating self-awareness, exploring our values and passions, and taking steps to express ourselves authentically, we can begin to live a more fulfilling, joyful, and purposeful life.

THE SUN

The Sun in astrology represents our core energy and our sense of self. Like the center of the solar system, it represents the center of your universe and the core of your identity. The sign the Sun is in (based on your birthday) reveals a lot about your natural energy: how you express yourself, what drives you, and what you want to be recognized for. Understanding and embracing your Sun sign energy can help you align with your authentic self and express yourself more confidently.

In a birth chart, the house that the Sun is in represents the area of life where you are most likely to express your sense of self and shine your brightest. You will spend your life growing into the highest expression of your Sun energy.

SUN = CONSCIOUS SELF
- Personal Power
- Ego
- Confidence
- Self-expression
- Creativity
- Best Self

The smallest of the zodiac constellations, Capricorn is bordered by the constellations Aquarius, Sagittarius, Microscopium, and Pisces. The constellation is relatively faint, with few bright stars, making it difficult to identify in the night sky. Its brightest star, called Deneb Algedi or Delta Capricorni, is a binary star system with a combined magnitude of 2.85.

The best time to view Capricorn in the night sky is during its culmination, which occurs around late August and early September. At that time, the constellation reaches its highest point in the sky and is most visible. In general, Capricorn can be seen between July and October, especially from the Southern Hemisphere, but it may be more challenging to spot from higher northern latitudes due to its position close to the southern celestial horizon. To find Capricorn in the night sky, you can use the brighter neighboring constellations as guides.

SATURN

Saturn, known for embodying discipline, responsibility, and authority, is recognized as the ruling planet of Capricorn. Capricorn individuals frequently reflect these Saturnine traits, demonstrating a similar discipline, sense of responsibility, and aspiration for authority. Saturn is also linked with the notion of time, the importance of structure and organization, and the inevitable experience of challenges and limitations. Capricorns, in alignment with these Saturnian principles, often encounter obstacles or delays on their life's journey. Yet, they typically overcome these hurdles with resilience, determination, and a pragmatic mindset, propelling them towards success.

The ruling planet of a zodiac sign is considered to be the planet that has the most influence over that sign's energy profile, because the ruling planet is believed to represent the energies and qualities that are most closely aligned with the sign's nature. Knowledge of the ruling planet can provide insight into the core energy and areas of growth of a sign. Understanding the ruling planet can provide guidance for working with the energies of a sign in a positive and productive way and can be used to enhance personal growth and self-awareness.

Earth signs focus on the physical world and the manifestation of tangible results. Taurus' role is to ground and embody stability, sensuality, and material abundance. Virgo's role is to analyze, refine, and improve. Capricorn's role is to embody ambition, responsibility, and structured progress.

EARTH SIGN ENERGY

TAURUS  VIRGO  CAPRICORN

PRACTICAL: Earth signs are known for their down-to-earth and practical approach to life. They are level-headed, realistic, and logical.

STABLE: Earth signs are known for their stability and dependability. They provide a grounding influence in any situation and are not easily swayed.

RELIABLE: Earth signs are dependable, trustworthy and responsible. People know they can count on them to be there when they are needed.

HARDWORKING: Earth signs are hardworking and diligent. They work tirelessly to achieve their goals.

> I am grounded, stable, and focused on manifesting my goals with practicality and persistence.

Capricorn tends to be more focused on the big picture and long-term goals, than the other earth signs, Taurus and Virgo.

INFLEXIBLE: Earth signs can be inflexible and may struggle with change. They may be resistant to trying new things or adapting to different situations.

STUBBORN: Earth signs can be stubborn, and may find it difficult to change their minds once they have made a decision.

TOO MATERIALISTIC: Earth signs may be overly focused on material wealth and success, to the point of neglecting other important aspects of life.

TOO SERIOUS: Earth signs can be overly serious and may struggle to relax and have fun.

GROUNDING EARTH

- Practice mindfulness and meditation to calm the mind and reduce stress.
- Engage in physical activities, such as yoga, hiking, or gardening, to help ground and balance their energy.
- Connect with nature, either through spending time outdoors or bringing natural elements into your environment.
- Incorporate aromatherapy, crystals, or essential oils into your daily routine.

CAPRICORN SUN VIBES

Capricorn Sun expresses cardinal energy in the physical world. They are ambitious and disciplined. Their goal is to embody awareness of the physical world and lead through achievement and recognition.

ARIES

CANCER

LIBRA

CAPRICORN

Initiative: Cardinal signs are known for taking the lead and starting new projects. They have a lot of energy and drive to get things done.

Adaptability: Cardinal signs are quick to adjust to changing circumstances and are often good problem solvers.

Ambition: They are highly motivated and have a strong desire to succeed in their goals.

Resourcefulness: They are practical and resourceful, able to find innovative solutions to problems.

CARDINAL
SIGN ENERGY

Cardinal energy has strong leadership qualities and focuses on individual direction.

CARDINAL SIGN ENERGY

Impatient: Can act impulsively, making decisions without fully considering the consequences.

Overly Competitive: Can become overly competitive and push themselves too hard.

Overly Confident: Can be overly self-assured and may underestimate the challenges they face.

Difficulty with Follow-Through: Sometimes take on too much at once, leading to exhaustion or burnout.

ARIES CANCER LIBRA CAPRICORN

CAPRICORN SUN VIBES

EMOTIONALLY TUNED IN

Energy is a fundamental force that is responsible for creating and sustaining movement, activity, and life. In the context of emotions, thoughts, and behaviors, energy can be thought of as a vibrational frequency. Different emotions, thoughts, and behaviors can be associated with different frequencies of energy.

High vibrational energy is associated with positive emotions, thoughts, and behaviors. People with high vibrational energy tend to be optimistic, compassionate, and empathetic. They are open to new experiences, and approach life with a sense of curiosity and wonder. High vibrational energy can have a positive impact on an individual's life. It can help them to attract positive experiences and opportunities, cultivate better relationships, and promote greater well-being. People with high vibrational energy tend to be happier, more fulfilled, and more successful in life.

HIGH FREQUENCY
Love   Joy   Gratitude
Forgiveness   Compassion   Empathy
Open-mindedness   Creativity
Inspiration   Curiosity

LOW FREQUENCY
Fear   Anger   Resentment   Jealousy
Envy   Cynicism   Skepticism   Pessimism
Judgmental   Closed-mindedness

Low vibrational energy, on the other hand, is associated with negative emotions, thoughts, and behaviors. People with low vibrational energy tend to be pessimistic, judgmental, and closed-minded. They may be resistant to change and approach life with a sense of cynicism and skepticism. Low vibrational energy can limit an individual's potential and lead to negative outcomes. It can contribute to feelings of stress, anxiety, and depression, and may lead to strained relationships and missed opportunities.

Everyone has good days and bad days. Remember, raising your vibration does not mean ignoring or suppressing your emotions but rather acknowledging and processing them in a healthy way. By processing and releasing negative emotions, you create space for positive emotions and higher frequencies to flow into your life.

HOW TO RAISE YOUR VIBRATION

1 Gratitude journaling: Each day, write down three things you are grateful for. This can help shift your focus towards the positive things in your life and promote feelings of joy and contentment.

2 Meditation: Spend 10-15 minutes each day in meditation, focusing on your breath and letting go of negative thoughts and emotions. This can help you feel more calm and centered, and promote greater well-being.

3 Acts of kindness: Engage in acts of kindness towards others, such as helping a neighbor with groceries or sending a thoughtful message to a friend. This can help promote feelings of compassion and empathy, and contribute to a more positive outlook on life.

4 Affirmations: Repeat positive affirmations to yourself throughout the day, such as "I am worthy of love and happiness" or "I trust in the universe to guide me towards my highest good". This can help shift your mindset towards a more positive and optimistic outlook.

What emotions do you experience most frequently?

What thoughts or behaviors do you engage in that may be limiting your potential?

What are some areas of your life where you feel stuck or stagnant, and how can you shift your energy towards a more positive direction?

How can you cultivate more positive emotions, thoughts, and behaviors in your daily life?

CAPRICORN SUN VIBES

When we operate from a higher expression of our natural energy, we are more likely to experience positive thoughts, emotions, and behaviors.

Capricorn sun energy

AMBITIOUS
Capricorns are driven and goal-oriented.

DISCIPLINED
Capricorns are focused and committed.

RESPONSIBLE
Capricorns are dependable and trustworthy.

PRACTICAL
Capricorns are realistic and pragmatic.

RESOURCEFUL
Capricorns are inventive and capable.

Sun energy represents our core identity, what we stand for, and what we aim to achieve in life. When your sun energy is positive, you embody qualities that help you manifest your goals and desires. This energy is in alignment with your authentic self and brings you joy and fulfillment.

Capricorn

Capricorn Energy
AMBITIOUS

Setting goals and working to achieve them

Highly driven in personal and professional pursuits

Capricorns are highly ambitious and strive to achieve their goals. They are focused and dedicated in their pursuits and are willing to put in the hard work and effort required to succeed.

You cannot climb a tree without bending some branches.

~African Proverb

What are some long-term goals that you have set for yourself?

CAPRICORN SUN VIBES

my VISION BOARD

Step 1: Identify Specific Goals
Step 2: Choose Images or Words that Represent Goals
Step 3: Arrange Images and Words on the Vision Board

Physical:

Spiritual:

Mental:

Relationships:

Professional:

Financial:

Travel and Recreational

Step 4: Identify Specific Steps to Achieve Goals (Use the Goals Planner on page 21 for this.)

By creating a visual representation of your goals, you can stay motivated and focused on achieving those goals.

Knock Your Goals Out the Park

Breaking down a big goal into smaller tasks can make it feel less overwhelming and more achievable.

1 Write down your goal.

2 Brainstorm smaller tasks that will need to happen to achieve your goal. Try to break the goal down into as many small tasks as you can.

3 Put the tasks in the correct order you will need to complete them. This will help you see the logical order of the tasks.

4 Set a deadline for each task. This will help you stay on track and make progress towards your goal.

5 Track your progress As you complete each task, check it off on the worksheet. This will help you see your progress and stay motivated.

GOAL PLANNER

- **1** Description
- **2** Inspiration
- **3** Task / Due Date
- **4** (Due Date column)
- **5** (Task rows)
- Notes

Now, use the planner on the next page for one of your goals on the vision board from earlier.

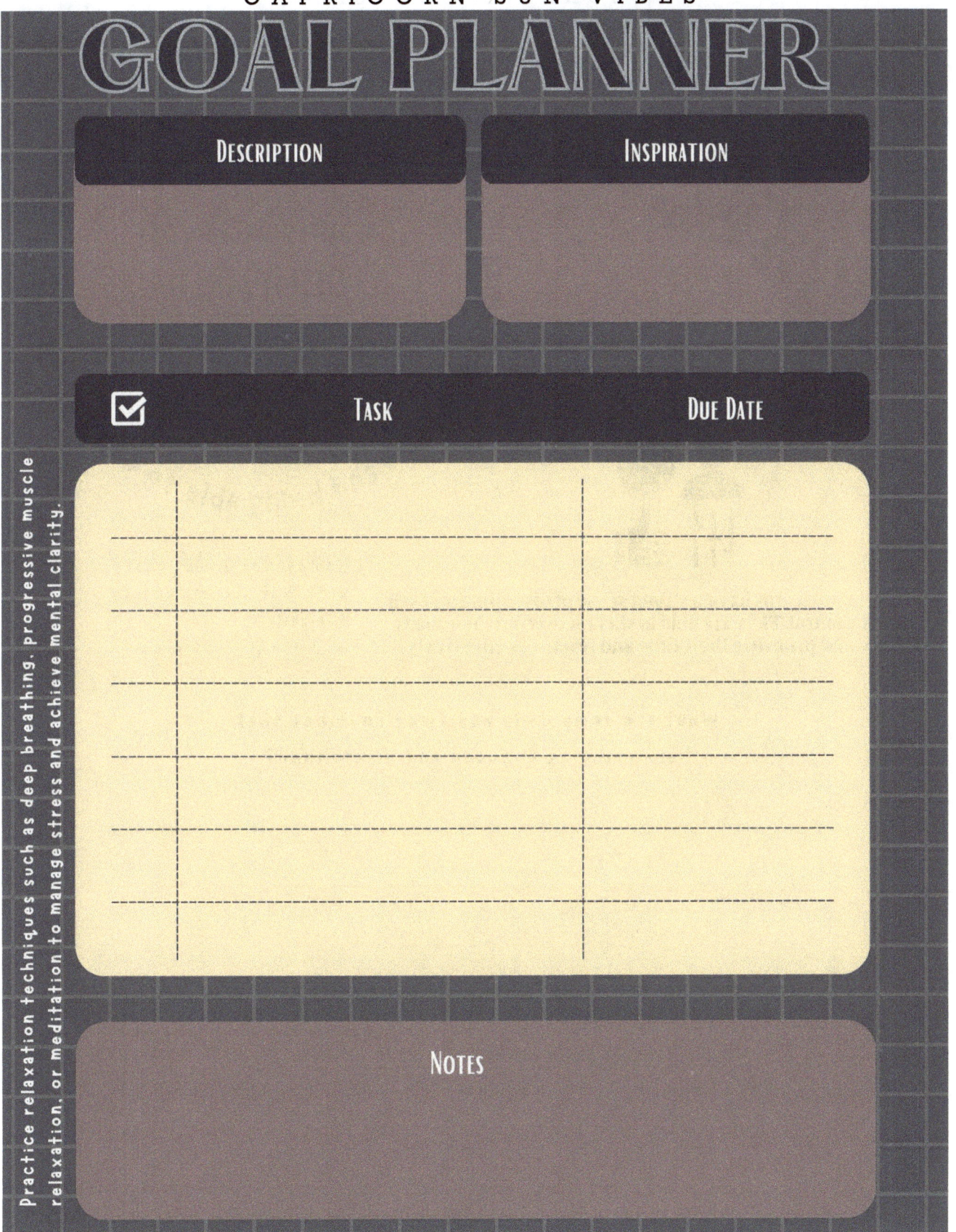

CAPRICORN SUN VIBES

GOAL PLANNER

Description

Inspiration

☑ **Task** **Due Date**

Notes

Practice relaxation techniques such as deep breathing, progressive muscle relaxation, or meditation to manage stress and achieve mental clarity.

Capricorn

Sticking to a regular routine or schedule

Prioritizing tasks and being able to delay gratification

Capricorn Energy
DISCIPLINED

Capricorns have a strong sense of discipline and self-control. They are able to stay focused on their goals and prioritize their time and resources effectively.

You cannot direct the wind, but you can adjust the sails.
~African Proverb

What are some daily habits or routines that help you stay focused and disciplined?

CAPRICORN SUN VIBES

WORK SMARTER, NOT HARDER
DELEGATE

10 TIPS On How To Delegate Effectively

1. Choose the right tasks to delegate
2. Provide clear instructions
3. Communicate expectations
4. Provide resources
5. Check in regularly
6. Trust your team
7. Follow up
8. Recognize and reward
9. Learn from mistakes
10. Be flexible

You are the manager of a small team that is responsible for developing a new product. One team member is a software developer who is responsible for writing the code for the product. She is a highly skilled developer and has been working on this project for several months. She is now starting to fall behind schedule and is struggling to keep up with the workload. Should you delegate some of her tasks to other team members?

You are the manager of a small team that is responsible for developing a new software application. One team member is a highly skilled programmer who is responsible for writing the code for the application. However, the software is very complex and requires a high level of expertise. The programmer is the only person on the team with the required skillset and knowledge to complete the project. Should you delegate some of her tasks to other team members?

You are the director of a non-profit organization that is responsible for organizing a large fundraising event. One of your team members is responsible for coordinating the catering for the event. She is very organized and detail-oriented, but has a lot on her plate. Should you delegate some of her responsibilities to another team member?

Organize your schedule to ensure that you allocate time for self-care and leisure activities, in addition to work and personal responsibilities.

FILL EACH DAY WITH

3 SMALL THINGS I APPRECIATE TODAY

3 GOOD THINGS THAT HAPPENED TODAY

TODAY'S POSITIVE AFFIRMATION

MY FAVORITE MOMENTS OF THE DAY

I am grateful for all the abundance and blessings in my life, and I open my heart to receive even more.

CAPRICORN SUN VIBES

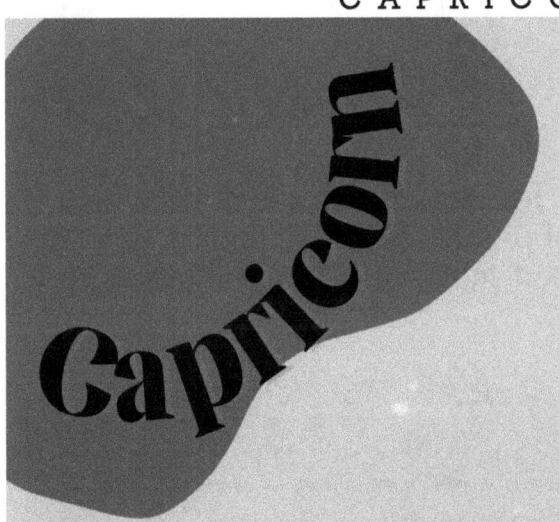

Capricorn Energy
RESPONSIBLE

Reliable and accountable for one's actions and commitments

Takes ownership of one's mistakes

Capricorns are known for their sense of responsibility and reliability. They take their commitments seriously and are often seen as the dependable ones in their personal and professional lives.

Do not look where you fell, but where you slipped.
~African Proverb

Role Play Scenario: Imagine you have been given a task that requires a high level of responsibility. How can you demonstrate that you are trustworthy and dependable in completing the task?

Hold Yourself Accountable

Taking accountability for our actions and commitments is an important part of personal growth and success. It can help us stay focused, motivated, and make progress towards our goals.

Section 1: Identify Areas of Responsibility

What are some areas of your life where you need to take more responsibility? What are some consequences of not taking responsibility in these areas?

By taking ownership of our actions and commitments, we can develop a greater sense of self-awareness and achieve our personal and professional goals.

Section 2: Set Specific Goals

What are some specific goals you want to achieve in these areas?
What are some potential obstacles that may prevent you from achieving these goals?
What are some strategies you can use to overcome these obstacles?

Section 3: Track Progress

What are some specific actions you can take to track your progress towards your goals? How often will you check in on your progress? What are some potential rewards or consequences for meeting or not meeting your goals?

CAPRICORN SUN VIBES

Capricorn

Capricorn Energy
PRACTICAL

Grounded in reality and using common sense to solve problems

Prioritizing function in decision-making

Capricorns are practical and grounded in reality. They are able to see things clearly and make sound judgments based on facts and evidence, rather than letting emotions or personal biases cloud their judgment.

Smooth seas do not make skillful sailors.
~African Proverb

What are some of the practical skills and abilities that you would like to develop, and what steps can you take to start building these skills?

RISING ABOVE DISAPPOINTMENT

In general, experiencing "failure" means something goes wrong or does not go according to plan. Think back to a time when something that was important to you did not go your way. What words come to mind as you think about this situation?

What feelings come to mind as you recall this situation?

What are some things you learned from this situation?

How can the things you learned be helpful in the future?

Now, you've turned that loss into a future win!

Learn to treat yourself with kindness and understanding to maintain a healthy mindset and find balance.

CAPRICORN SUN VIBES

What are some new strategies you can use to approach future challenges?

How can you incorporate these strategies into your daily life?

What are some potential benefits and drawbacks of these strategies?

Remember that facing challenges is a natural part of life, and by developing new strategies, you can learn from these experiences and become a stronger and more resilient person.

In the face of adversity, I am resilient and strong. Each challenge I meet is an opportunity for growth, shaping me into a stronger and wiser version of myself.

Capricorn

Capricorn Energy
RESOURCEFUL

Using creativity and innovative thinking to find solutions to problems

Adaptable to achieve goals

Capricorns are resourceful and are often able to find solutions to problems that others may not have considered. They are able to think outside the box and find innovative ways to overcome obstacles.

When spider webs unite, they can tie up a lion.

~African Proverb

How have you used your resourcefulness to solve a problem in the past?

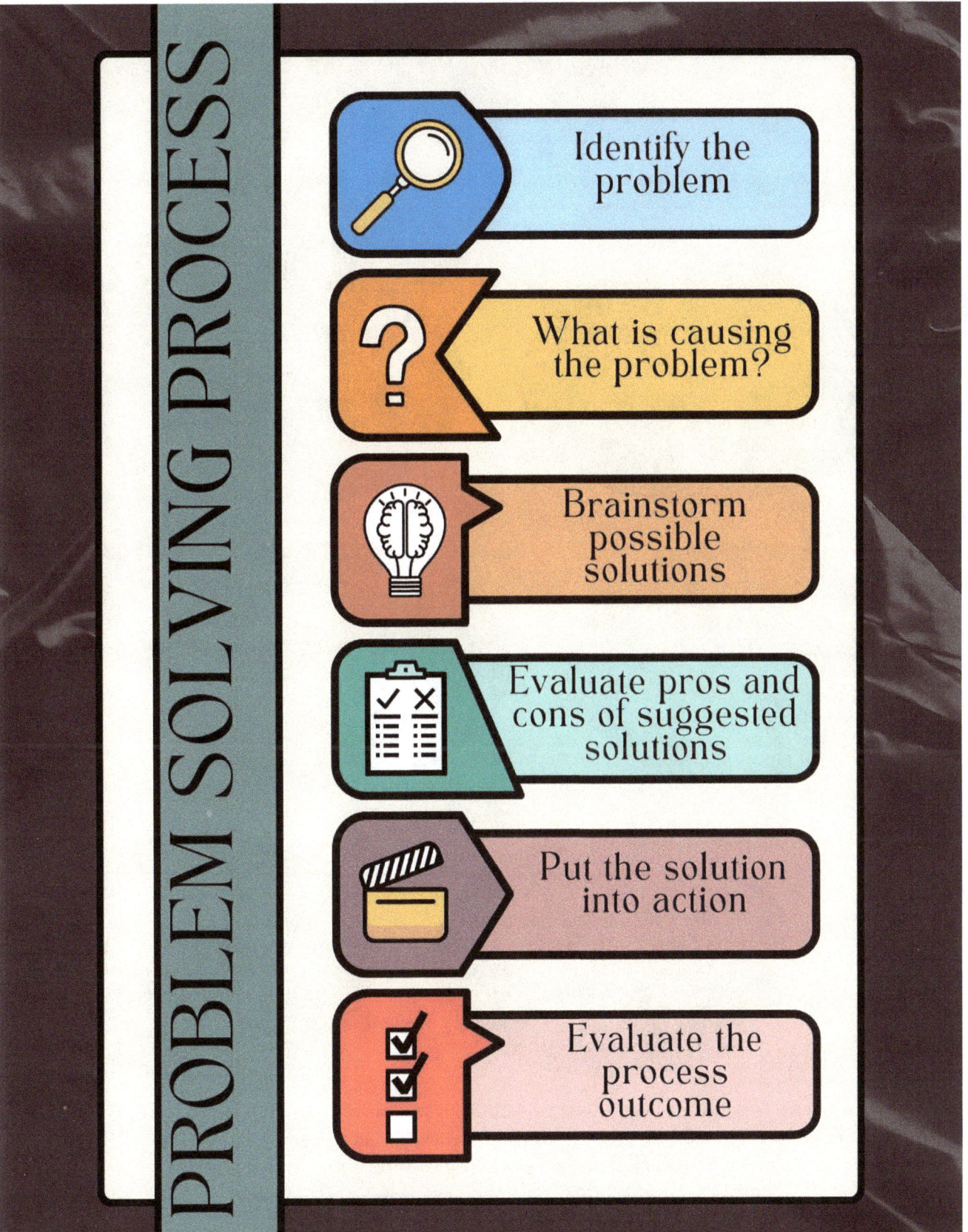

LOOKING FOR ANSWERS!

Can you come up with creative and innovative solutions for each problem.

- Your school has a limited budget for extracurricular activities, and the students are frustrated with the lack of options.

- Your local food bank is experiencing a shortage of donations, and there is a high demand for food assistance among community members.

- Your community is experiencing an increase in traffic congestion and pollution, and residents are concerned about the impact on the environment and quality of life.

- Your school is experiencing a high rate of absenteeism, and it is affecting student achievement.

- Your school is struggling to provide inclusive education for students with disabilities, and there is a lack of resources and support for these students.

- Your workplace is experiencing a high turnover rate, and it is affecting productivity and morale.

Nurture and invest time in your personal connections, as they can often be a source of diverse ideas, perspectives, and skills. By leveraging these relationships, you can gain new insights and approaches to problem-solving, showcasing your resourcefulness in collaborative contexts.

1

Capricorn preschoolers may exhibit a serious and responsible demeanor, often taking on tasks and responsibilities beyond their years. They could be cautious and reserved, preferring to observe and analyze situations before acting.

2

Capricorn children in elementary school may show a love for learning and knowledge, often excelling in academics and extracurricular activities. They could be perfectionists and hard on themselves but also exhibit a strong sense of discipline and responsibility.

3

Capricorn children in their tween years may become more focused on achievement and success, with a desire to excel in academics or other areas of interest. They could also become more self-conscious and sensitive to criticism and struggle with feelings of insecurity.

4

Capricorn teenagers may be highly ambitious and goal-oriented, with a drive to succeed in their chosen pursuits. They may become more independent and self-sufficient but also struggle with feelings of pressure or overwhelm. They could also be more critical of themselves and others and benefit from cultivating self-compassion and empathy.

5

Capricorn adults often exhibit a strong work ethic and a practical approach to life, with a focus on achieving their long-term goals and aspirations. They may also have a strong sense of responsibility and duty and take on leadership roles or positions of authority. They could benefit from cultivating a balance between work and personal life and from learning to express their emotions and vulnerability in a healthy way.

CAPRICORN SUN VIBES

Be Mindful

> Mindfulness is a practice of being fully present and engaged in the current moment.

Mindfulness can increase self-awareness and promote emotional regulation. When we are more aware of our thoughts and emotions, we can respond to triggers in a more constructive way, rather than allowing them to control our actions. Mindfulness practices teach us to be present in the moment and accepting things as they are, rather than always seeking immediate gratification or trying to control outcomes. Over time, regular mindfulness practice can help us develop greater mental clarity and emotional resilience, allowing us to remain calm and centered even in the face of intense emotion.

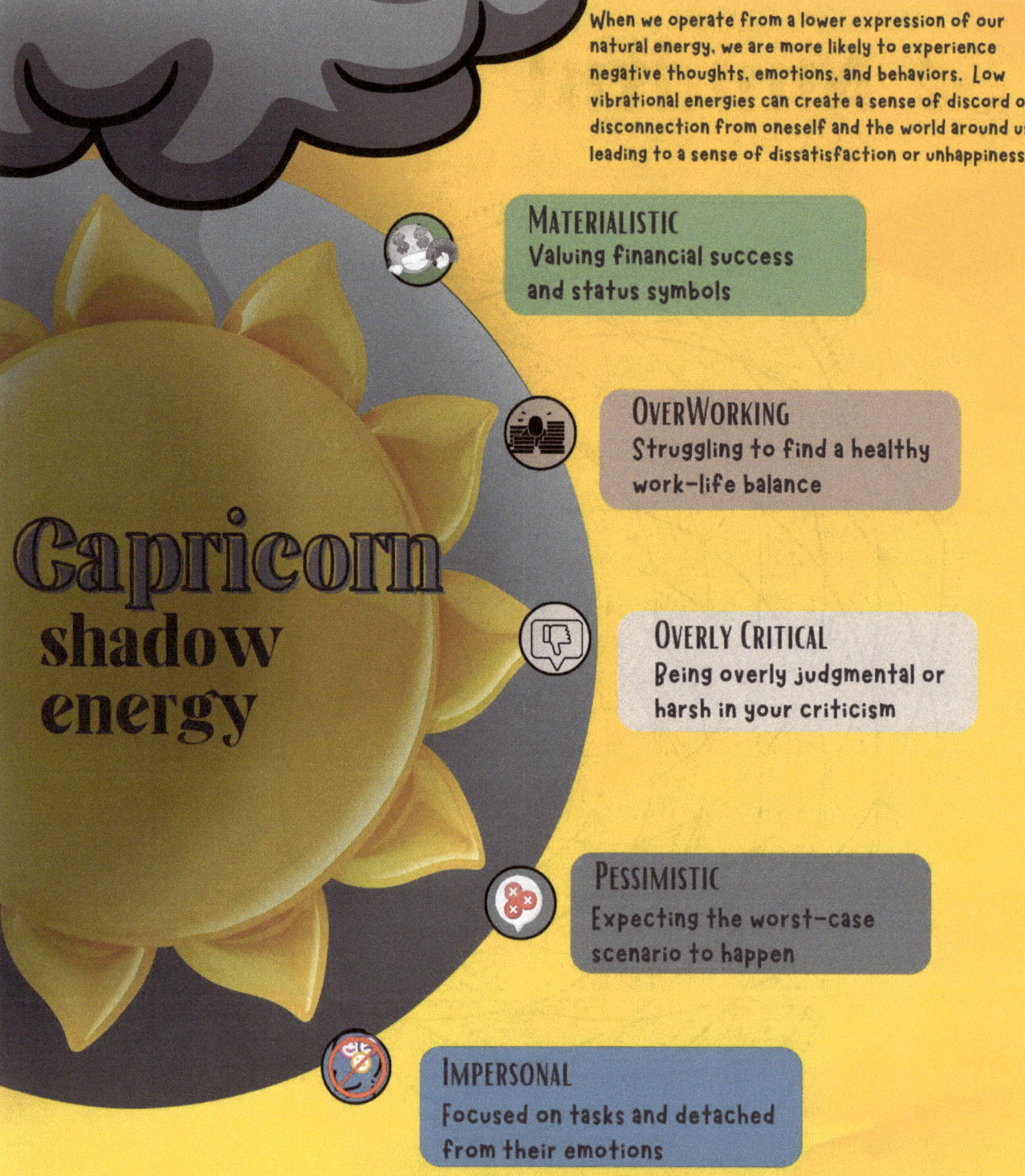

When we operate from a lower expression of our natural energy, we are more likely to experience negative thoughts, emotions, and behaviors. Low vibrational energies can create a sense of discord or disconnection from oneself and the world around us, leading to a sense of dissatisfaction or unhappiness.

Capricorn shadow energy

MATERIALISTIC
Valuing financial success and status symbols

OVERWORKING
Struggling to find a healthy work-life balance

OVERLY CRITICAL
Being overly judgmental or harsh in your criticism

PESSIMISTIC
Expecting the worst-case scenario to happen

IMPERSONAL
Focused on tasks and detached from their emotions

When sun energy is in shadow, it manifests negative energy. This shadow energy often stems from unresolved issues or insecurities. Recognizing and accepting the shadow of one's sun energy can help to integrate these aspects. Using tools and methods at your disposal will allow you to transform this negative energy into positive, thereby enhancing overall well-being.

CAPRICORN SUN VIBES

Capricorn

Shadow Energy: MATERIALISTIC

In their shadow, Capricorns can be focused on material success and may place too much emphasis on money and material possessions.

Practice: GRATITUDE

Role Play Scenario: Play the role of a wealthy businessperson who values their possessions over their relationships. Reflect on how your actions impact your relationships and your own personal growth.

SHONETTE CHARLES

Treasures and Memories

Make a list of all the possessions you currently own and memorable experiences you've had. Estimate the true value of each possession, including the financial cost, time cost, and an estimate of the emotional value.

POSSESSIONS	VALUE	EXPERIENCES	VALUE

CAPRICORN SUN VIBES

Inventory Analysis

By taking stock of your possessions and evaluating their true value and importance, you can prioritize what truly matters and make more intentional decisions about how you spend your time, money, and energy.

> What things on each list mean more to you? Which list has more things of high value?

> What things have lost value over time? Which list has more of these items?

> What did you learn from this inventory exercise?

Remember that possessions can play an important role in our lives, but they should not define our happiness or our sense of self-worth.

Capricorn

Shadow Energy: OVERWORKING

In their shadow, Capricorns can be workaholics and may struggle to find a healthy work-life balance. They may push themselves too hard and neglect their personal lives and relationships.

Practice: BOUNDARIES

Write about a time when you felt like you were working too much. How did it impact your personal life and relationships?

CAPRICORN SUN VIBES

A TALE OF TWO STUDENTS

LaToya was a college student with big dreams. She was studying pre-med and was determined to become a doctor. She spent most of her days in the library, studying and doing research. She was always busy, always working, and always stressed. She had no time for fun or relaxation. Her friends invited her to parties, but she always declined, saying she had too much work to do.

LaToya had no balance in her life. She was so focused on her studies and her future career that she had no time for anything else. She didn't exercise, didn't eat well, and didn't socialize. She was always tired and irritable.

One day, LaToya realized that she had missed out on a lot of experiences in college. She had no memories of parties or late-night conversations with friends. She realized that all her hard work was making her miserable. She decided that she needed to make a change.

LaToya started by scheduling time for self-care. She made sure to get enough sleep, exercise, and eat well. She also started saying yes to invitations from friends. She realized that taking time to have fun and socialize actually made her more productive and less stressed. She was able to focus better on her studies and her future career when she had a healthy work-life balance.

Kyan was a college student who was struggling to find his balance. He spent most of his days partying and socializing with friends. He was always looking for the next big event or activity to attend. He barely had time for studying, and when he did, he was too tired or hungover to focus.

Kyan had no balance in his life. He was so focused on having fun and being social that he had no time for anything else. He didn't take his studies seriously and was in danger of failing his classes.

One day, Kyan realized that he was not making the most of his college experience. He was missing out on the opportunity to learn and grow. He decided that he needed to make a change.

Kyan started by scheduling time for studying. He made sure to attend all his classes and to spend time in the library. He also started saying no to invitations from friends when he had studying to do. He realized that taking time to focus on his studies actually made him feel better and more productive. He was able to enjoy his social life more when he knew he had taken care of his responsibilities.

Kyan's new balance helped him succeed in college and in life. He became more focused and confident. He was able to have fun and socialize with friends, but he also took his studies seriously.

What are the risks of being too focused on work or academics and neglecting personal well-being?

What are the risks of being too focused on socializing and neglecting academic responsibilities?

What are the benefits of having a healthy work-life balance?

What changes can you make to prioritize your well-being and find a healthier work-life balance?

SHONETTE CHARLES

Self-Care Planner

TOP 3 SELF-CARE PRIORITIES

-
-
-

SELF-CARE ACTIVITIES

AFFIRMATIONS

DAILY WATER TRACKER

NOTES

I honor my commitment to a balanced life, understanding that self-care is essential to my overall success and happiness.

30-DAY SELF-CARE *Challenge*

DAY 1	DAY 2	DAY 3	DAY 4	DAY 5
Go on a Leisurely Walk Alone	Declutter 10 Items	Create a Vision Board	Be Good to Someone You Love	Start a New Inspiring Book
DAY 6	**DAY 7**	**DAY 8**	**DAY 9**	**DAY 10**
Get a Massage	Detox From Social Media	Do a Random Act of Kindness	Hydrate with 8 glasses of water	Commit to a Day of Eating Healthy
DAY 11	**DAY 12**	**DAY 13**	**DAY 14**	**DAY 15**
Try Something New	Find a Quiet Spot and Read	Get an Extra Hour of Sleep	Create a Fitness Goal	Meditate for 10 Minutes
DAY 16	**DAY 17**	**DAY 18**	**DAY 19**	**DAY 20**
Create a Morning Routine	Unplug for 12 hours	Do something spontaneous	Skip the Added Sugar	Write 3 Intentions for Yourself
DAY 21	**DAY 22**	**DAY 23**	**DAY 24**	**DAY 25**
Create a Bedtime Routine	Start Your Day With Gratitude	Identify Three Stressors	Send a "Thank You" Note	Engage in Self-Reflection
DAY 26	**DAY 27**	**DAY 28**	**DAY 29**	**DAY 30**
Take a personal day	Call a friend	Give Yourself a Daily Facial	Watch sunset or sunrise	Make a Wish

You don't have to do these in order. Just do them!

Capricorn

Shadow Energy: OVERLY CRITICAL

In their shadow, Capricorns can be very self-critical and may hold themselves and others to excessively high standards.

Practice: EMPATHY

Role Play Scenario: Play the role of an overly critical boss or leader. Reflect on the impact that your criticism has on your team's morale, motivation, and productivity.

CAPRICORN SUN VIBES

Energy Crush

Identify people in your life who you admire or respect, such as friends, family members, or colleagues.

Write down the positive qualities you admire in others and why they are important to you.

Write the achievements that are most impressive and meaningful to you and why they inspire you.

Practice putting yourself in their shoes and seeing the world from their perspective. What did you learn?

By recognizing the good in others, you can develop deeper and more meaningful relationships with those around you, and inspire others to recognize the good in themselves.

THE *Gratitude* JAR

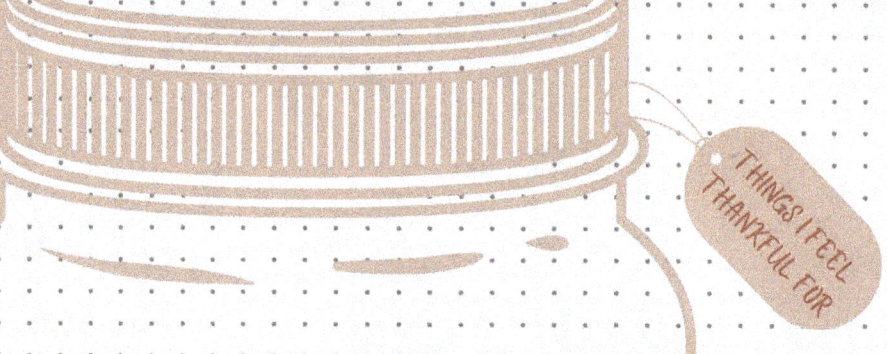

THINGS I FEEL THANKFUL FOR

Find a jar or box and decorate it however you like. Then, write down things that you are grateful for on small pieces of paper and put them in the jar or box. You can do this daily, weekly, or whenever you feel like it. Then, when you need a boost of positivity, you can read through the notes and be reminded of all the good things in your life.

CAPRICORN SUN VIBES

Capricorn

Shadow Energy: PESSIMISTIC

In their shadow, Capricorns can be overly focused on the negative and may struggle to see the positive aspects of a situation.

Practice: OPTIMISM

Consider a pattern of negative thinking that you often fall into (e.g. catastrophizing, black-and-white thinking, negative self-talk). How does this pattern of thinking impact your overall well-being and quality of life? What are some more positive or helpful alternatives to this pattern of thinking that you could start practicing instead? How might these new ways of thinking impact your life in a positive way?

SHONETTE CHARLES

Positive Spin

Our thoughts have a powerful impact on our emotions and behavior. Negative thinking patterns can lead to anxiety, stress, and depression. Reframing our thoughts and focusing on positive perspectives can help us build resilience and cope with life's challenges. This exercise will guide you through the process of identifying and reframing pessimistic thoughts to cultivate a more optimistic and hopeful mindset.

NEGATIVE THOUGHT	POSITIVE SPIN
I always fail.	
Nobody cares about me.	
Nothing ever goes right for me.	
I'll never be happy.	
I don't have enough time/money/resources.	
I'll never be able to do this.	
I'm not smart/talented/creative enough.	
I'm not worthy of love and acceptance.	
I'll never be successful.	
Everyone is better than me.	
I'm too old/young for this.	
I'll be stuck here forever.	

CAPRICORN SUN VIBES

Capricorn

Shadow Energy: Difficulty Expressing Emotion

In their shadow, Capricorns can be reserved and may have difficulty expressing their emotions.

Practice: Self Reflection

Write about a time when you struggled to express your emotions. What emotions were you feeling? Why do you think it was difficult to express them? Were there any particular thoughts, beliefs, or fears that were getting in the way? What could you have done differently to express your emotions more effectively in the moment?

MY FEELINGS

Feelings are physical sensations you feel in your body. Draw how it feels in your body when you are feeling each emotion.

HAPPY

SAD

CALM

FRUSTRATED

ANGRY

SCARED

Emotions are a natural part of the human experience, but many of us struggle to express them in healthy and productive ways. This exercise is designed to help you build awareness of your emotions and identify different ways to express them. By acknowledging and understanding your feelings, you can improve your emotional intelligence and build deeper and more meaningful connections with others.

CAPRICORN SUN VIBES

By learning to understand and express your emotions, you can build emotional intelligence, improve your personal and professional relationships, and lead a more fulfilling life. Don't let fear or discomfort hold you back. Take the time to reflect, practice, and grow, and you may be surprised at the positive impact it can have on your life.

I feel happy when...

Healthy Way to Express

I feel sad when...

Healthy Way to Express

I feel calm when...

Healthy Way to Express

I feel frustrated when...

Healthy Way to Express

I feel angry when...

Healthy Way to Express

I feel scared when...

Healthy Way to Express

Capricorns tend to be loyal and reliable friends who value trust and honesty in their relationships. They may be somewhat reserved and cautious when it comes to making new friends, but once they have established a close bond, they are committed and supportive.

Capricorn students tend to be serious and dedicated, with a strong desire to excel academically. They may be perfectionistic and hard on themselves but also have a strong sense of discipline and responsibility. They may benefit from cultivating a healthy balance between academic pursuits and other areas of interest.

FRIENDSHIP

SCHOOL

CAREER

FINANCES

Capricorns are often drawn to careers that allow them to demonstrate their strong work ethic and practical skills. They may excel in leadership roles or positions of authority, and may be highly ambitious and goal-oriented. They may benefit from cultivating a balance between work and personal life, and from learning to delegate and trust others to help them achieve their goals.

Capricorns tend to be practical and disciplined when it comes to managing their finances. They may be careful with their spending and value stability and security when it comes to their financial situation. They may also be highly ambitious when it comes to building wealth and be willing to take calculated risks to achieve their long-term financial goals.

What are some qualities you admire in a friend? How can you bring these qualities to your friendships as a Capricorn sun?

Research some stocks or industries you would like to invest in for the future.

Create a plan for how you will attain the necessary education or training for a successful career.

How can you use your Capricorn sun energy to excel in your studies or career?

Sun energy and shadow energy are different levels (high or low) of expression of the natural energy in your energy profile. The expression of your sun energy is aligned with your authentic self. Shadow energy, on the other hand, can be expressed when we are under stress or feel threatened. By recognizing and releasing low vibrational behavior, we can free ourselves from limiting beliefs, negative emotions, and self-defeating patterns, and open ourselves up to new possibilities, experiences, and ways of being by transmuting the shadow energy into sun energy.

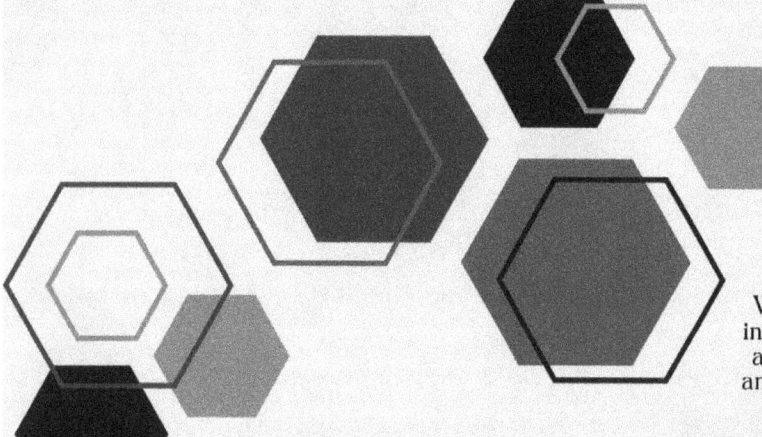

ENERGY FREQUENCY

Write each energy trait in the correct box. Which are the high expression and the low expression of the same energy?

transmute: change in nature

In order to transmute our shadow energy, it is helpful to identify the situations, beliefs, and triggers that activate it, as well as the emotions and needs that underlie it. This can involve practices such as mindfulness, journaling, and self-reflection. By identifying and replacing negative patterns that are holding us back, we convert them into more positive, life-affirming ones. Overall, the process of transmuting shadow energy into sun energy is an ongoing one that requires self-awareness, self-compassion, and intentional effort. By recognizing and transforming our shadow energy, we can develop a deeper understanding of ourselves, increase our self-awareness, and cultivate greater fulfillment, purpose, and joy in our lives.

HIGH

disciplined   pessimist
difficulty expressing emotion
responsible   materialistic   practical
overly critical   overworked
ambitious   resourceful

LOW

CAPRICORN SUN VIBES

Motivation
Ambitious vs Materialistic

AMBITIOUS
- Strong desire to achieve one's goals and succeed in life
- Recognizes the value of things other than material goods

Find a quiet and comfortable place to sit or stand. Close your eyes, and focus your attention on your breath. Take slow, deep breaths in through your nose, and out through your mouth. As you breathe, notice the sensation of the air moving in and out of your body.

MATERIALISTIC
- Excessive focus on material possessions and wealth
- Views material things as the ultimate measure of success

Reflect on your ambitions and consider whether they are driven by a desire for personal growth and meaningful achievement, or primarily by the pursuit of material wealth. How might aligning your aspirations with deeper values and purpose influence your path to success?

> My ambition fuels my journey towards purpose and personal growth, not just material wealth.

CAPRICORN SUN VIBES

Disciplined

- Ability to control one's behavior and maintain focus on one's goals

- Committed and dedicated

VS

Overworking

- Tendency to work excessively, often at the expense of other important aspects of life

- Lacking work-life balance

Engage in creative activities like drawing, painting, writing, or playing music can be a great way to release stress and reconnect with ourselves. Set aside some time each day or week to explore a creative activity that you enjoy.

COMMITMENT TO WORK OR PRODUCTIVITY

"I am determined and persistent, but I am also open to new ideas and approaches.

How do you maintain the focus and consistency necessary for success without tipping over into the realm of overwork and potential burnout?

CAPRICORN SUN VIBES

HIGH STANDARDS AND EXPECTATIONS

Responsible

Sense of accountability and reliability in one's commitments and obligations

Realistic and steady progress to yield results

VS

Overly Critical

Tendency to be overly judgmental and negative, often towards oneself or others

Excessively harsh and unrealistic in judgments

> I find joy and fulfillment in the beauty of the world around me, and I am grateful for the sensory experiences in my life.

In what ways does my desire for material possessions impact my life and relationships?

Create a vision board that focuses on sensory experiences and beauty, rather than material possessions.

Resourceful

Ability to find creative and effective solutions to problems

Proactive and solution-oriented

Pessimistic

Tendency to focus on negative outcomes and possibilities, often to the detriment of positive ones.

Resigned or fatalistic in approach

> "My heart is open to new experiences and ideas."

perspective on challenges

In what ways have my loyal relationships positively impacted my life?

In what situations do you tend to be resistant to change, and how can you work to become more adaptable?

CAPRICORN SUN VIBES

PRACTICAL

Focus on the practical and tangible aspects of life

Rational and logical approach to problem-solving

Tendency to struggle with expressing one's feelings or emotional states

Uncomfortable with emotions

DIFFICULTY EXPRESSING EMOTION

I allow myself to express my feelings when appropriate and healthy.

RESERVED EMOTIONS

In what areas of your life do you tend to be closed-minded, and how can you work to be more open-minded?

Make a list of things you're curious about, and choose one to explore in more depth.

Capricorn

1st House (Self): Capricorn sun in the 1st house can indicate a serious, responsible, and practical approach to life. The individual may be perceived as a hard worker and a leader and have a reserved or stoic demeanor.

Capricorn Sun In the Houses

2nd House (Values and Possessions): Capricorn sun in the 2nd house can indicate a strong desire for financial stability and security, as well as a practical and methodical approach to managing resources. The individual may place a high value on hard work and material success.

3rd House (Communication and Immediate Environment): Capricorn sun in the 3rd house can indicate a serious and disciplined approach to communication and learning. The individual may be an excellent teacher or student, with a gift for practical and logical thinking.

4th House (Home and Family): Capricorn sun in the 4th house can indicate a strong sense of responsibility towards family and a desire for security and stability in the home. The individual may have a traditional approach to family life and prioritize career and financial success in order to provide for their loved ones.

5th House (Creativity and Self-Expression): Capricorn sun in the 5th house can indicate a serious and disciplined approach to creative expression and self-identity. The individual may have a reserved or controlled expression of their emotions and may approach romance and leisure activities in a practical and responsible manner.

6th House (Work and Health): Capricorn sun in the 6th house can indicate a strong work ethic and a desire for practical and productive employment. The individual may take a disciplined approach to maintaining physical and mental health and value routine and structure in their daily life.

7th House (Relationships): Capricorn sun in the 7th house can indicate a serious and responsible approach to partnerships and relationships. The individual may seek out partners who share their values and work ethic and place a high value on long-term commitment and stability in relationships.

8th House (Intimacy and Transformation): Capricorn sun in the 8th house can indicate a serious and disciplined approach to transformation and personal growth. The individual may be focused on achieving power and status through hard work and be interested in pursuing financial investments or other ways to build wealth.

9th House (Expansion and Higher Learning): Capricorn sun in the 9th house can indicate a serious and disciplined approach to travel and philosophical pursuits. The individual may be drawn to traditional or conservative approaches to spirituality and value practical and useful knowledge.

10th House (Career and Public Life): Capricorn sun in the 10th house can indicate a strong desire for success and recognition in the public sphere. The individual may have a serious and disciplined approach to career and value traditional or conservative values in the workplace.

11th House (Community and Networking): Capricorn sun in the 11th house can indicate a disciplined and methodical approach to social groups and personal aspirations. The individual may value connections with people who share their goals and approach social interactions in a reserved or controlled manner.

12th House (Subconscious and Hidden Matters): Capricorn sun in the 12th house can indicate a serious and disciplined approach to exploring the hidden or spiritual realms. The individual may be drawn to traditional or conservative spiritual practices and have a reserved or controlled expression of their emotions. They could also have a tendency towards self-criticism and self-doubt.

CAPRICORN SUN VIBES

Gardening
Stimulates the flow of energy

Choose a suitable location or container for your garden.
Select plants or seeds that resonate with you and are appropriate for your growing conditions.
Prepare the soil, plant your seeds or plants, and provide them with the necessary water and care.
As you tend to your garden, focus on the connection between your hands, the earth, and the plants.
Observe the growth and transformation of your plants over time, reflecting on the lessons they teach about patience and nurturing.

Grounding Meditation
Calms the mind and balances the flow of energy

Find a quiet, comfortable place to sit or stand, preferably outdoors or on a natural surface.
Close your eyes and take a few deep breaths to center yourself.
Visualize roots extending from the soles of your feet, connecting you deeply to the earth.
As you inhale, imagine drawing energy and nourishment from the earth. As you exhale, release any tension or negative energy into the ground.
Continue this visualization for 5-10 minutes, then gently return your awareness to the present moment.

Forest Bathing
Removes negative energy

Choose a nearby forest, park, or natural area to explore.
Set aside at least an hour for your forest bathing experience.
Walk slowly and mindfully through the forest, focusing on the sensation of each step. As you walk, focus on the feeling of your feet connecting with the earth and imagine yourself rooting down with each step.
Pause periodically to observe the sights, sounds, smells, and sensations around you.
At the end of your walk, take a few moments to reflect on your experience and the insights gained.

Earth Shield
Promotes a sense of safety and security

Find a quiet, comfortable place to sit or stand.
Close your eyes and take a few deep breaths to center yourself.
Visualize a sphere of solid, protective earth energy surrounding you, like a protective barrier.
Imagine this barrier repelling negative energies and providing a stable foundation.

Creative · Mindfulness · Protecting · Cleansing

HEALING *Gratitude*

Stress Relief   **Improve Mental Clarity**   **Greater Perspective**

Expressing gratitude connects me to my authentic self, allowing me to find healing, grounding, and a deeper appreciation for the journey of life.

Practice gratitude by making a list of things you're thankful for each day, which can help you maintain a sense of perspective and positivity.

Capricorn Through the Planets

Capricorn Sun: A serious and responsible approach to life, with a desire for financial stability and a traditional approach to family and relationships.

Capricorn Moon: Reserved and controlled expression of emotions, with a need for stability and security in relationships and a tendency towards self-criticism and doubt.

Capricorn Mercury: Practical and methodical approach to communication and learning, with a disciplined and serious attitude towards knowledge and information.

Capricorn Saturn: A disciplined and serious approach to responsibility and hard work, with a desire for financial stability and a traditional approach to authority and social structure.

Capricorn Neptune: A desire for spiritual and emotional fulfillment within a traditional and structured framework, with a disciplined and serious approach to creativity and inspiration.

Capricorn Rising: An individual who presents a reserved, serious, and disciplined exterior to the world, with a strong work ethic and a focus on practical and traditional values.

Capricorn Pluto: A desire for power and transformation through hard work and discipline, with a traditional and serious approach to personal growth and regeneration.

Capricorn Venus: A traditional and reserved approach to love and relationships, with a need for stability and security in partnerships and a desire for financial success.

Capricorn Jupiter: A desire for traditional values and a methodical approach to personal growth and expansion, with a strong work ethic and a focus on achieving success and recognition.

Capricorn Mars: A disciplined and hard-working approach to achieving goals and pursuing success, with a tendency towards emotional control and a desire for material success.

Capricorn Uranus: A desire for change and innovation within a traditional and structured framework, with a disciplined and practical approach to personal freedom and individuality.

CAPRICORN

How have the insights in this journal shifted your perspective about your strengths, challenges, and approach to life?

What strategies are you most eager to apply to help you transmute shadow energy?

How will understanding your sun sign energy better contribute to your future growth and success?

www.ingramcontent.com/pod-product-compliance
Lightning Source LLC
Chambersburg PA
CBHW050456110426
42743CB00017B/3384